FREE JUMPING – A PRACTICAL HANDBOOK

FREE JUMPING – A PRACTICAL HANDBOOK

GYMNASTIC WORK, TRAINING AND DEVELOPMENT

By Claudia Götz

Legal Disclaimer

The author, the publisher and any other persons directly or indirectly involved with this book are not responsible for any accident or injury occurring from following the instructions given in this manuscript.

When dealing with horses you must be aware of taking adequate safety measures such as wearing sensible footwear and gloves when working horses from the ground, and a safety riding helmet, riding boots, gloves and an appropriate body protector when riding.

Copyright of original edition © 2008 by Cadmos Verlag GmbH,
Im Dorfe 11, 22956 Brunsbek, Germany

Copyright of this edition © 2008 by Cadmos Books, Great Britain

Translation: Claire Lilley

Design and layout: Ravenstein + Partner

Cover photo: Maximilian Schreiner

Photos without copyright notice: Maximilian Schreiner

Editorial: Anneke Bosse, Christopher Long

Printed by: agensketterl Druckerei, Mauerbach

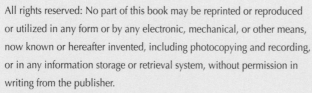

British Library Cataloguing in Publication Data

A catalogue record of this book is available from the British Library.

Printed in Austria

ISBN 978-3-86127-954-9

www.cadmos.co.uk

CONTENTS

An extremely talented horse amidst a veritable forest of jumps!
A familiar sight in the auction ring or at stallion displays.

WHY DO FREE JUMPING?

'Free jumping is only for professionals!' 'Only show jumpers should free-jump!' .
In fact, to free-jump all you need is a big indoor school, a lot of help and loads of jumps!

There are so many more uses for free jumping than you think. It is fascinating to find out what free jumping really is, what is involved and why it is beneficial to so many horses. Most people's idea of free jumping comes from photos in auction catalogues or of stallion displays.

It is easy to forget that these horses are young, talented and caught on camera at just the right moment to show them at their very best.

Talented horses can be of any breed. This coloured Irish mare shows outstanding jumping ability with her supple and elastic style. Even over a low jump she shows great front leg technique – comparable to what the Americans tend to look for in a hunter.

WHAT IS FREE JUMPING?

Generally speaking, free jumping is where the horse jumps without the rider. This can be carried out in various ways: leading in-hand, loose schooling with a team of whip-handlers or on the lunge. With free jumping many things are going on at different levels. Firstly it adds a different dimension to the horse's everyday training; free jumping improves the horse's dexterity and suppleness and it is often a way of developing self-confidence and courage. It can enhance your horse's jumping training and can be useful for correcting specific problems that can occur when jumping a course. Last but not least, it is a great way of introducing the horse to different obstacles and new jump fillers that it has not seen before.

Let's look at more specific aspects: you may ride for pleasure, or be an ambitious competitor. In either case, this usually takes the form of riding dressage in an arena, driving with a carriage, jumping, training for long distance riding or simply spending a lot of time hacking. Whatever your field of interest it goes without saying that introducing different types of work plays an important role in helping stimulate you and your horse to do better. Concentrating too much on one aspect can cause mental stress and early physical degeneration, such as wear and tear on specific muscle groups. It is not only young horses that need a good all-round education and different aspects to their work to keep them interested, older animals also appreciate variety.

Free jumping can be done in the paddock with very simple equipment. The rules for building jumps are the same as in the school. The height of the obstacles should be suitable for the horse, as seen here with this fjord pony. (Photo: Christiane Slawik)

With young horses it is very important to develop the small, deep muscles that connect to the skeleton and this is only possible through a training regime that encourages a wide range of movement in the body.

Too much repetition of the same work causes a lack of stimulus in the muscles and can result in uneven muscular development in the body, which can have a dramatic effect on the stability and function of the body as a whole. Over the last ten years young horses do not seem to have had the variety in their work that they used to, often resulting in degeneration of the vertebrae or kissing spines. The reverse could also be true: horses with kissing spines can develop specific problems when worked in a repetitive way. Nowadays there is a trend to

work talented young dressage horses exclusively in dressage work, whether they are ridden indoors or outside. It would do them so much good to include some hacking or free jumping in their training. Variety is good for mental development as well as physical and can give a new lease of life to experienced older horses, helping them to stay younger for longer. Psychological benefits can be an improvement in concentration and in learning ability. Horses are much more receptive to new exercises when an element of fun is brought into their work, making training more like a game than a chore. In general, even horses that are confident when hacking out will benefit from adding a new dimension to their training. This can all be achieved by including free jumping.

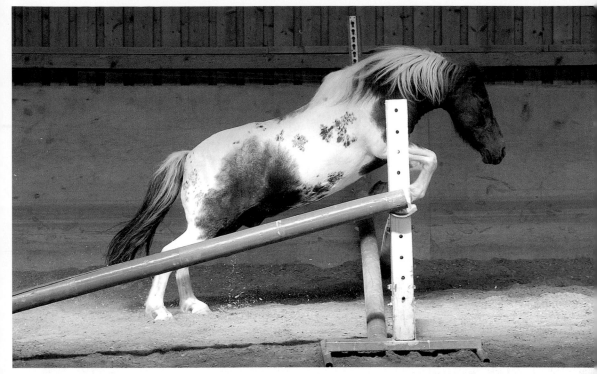

A Shetland can also have great fun free jumping. Obviously the distances between jumps in a grid must be carefully measured to fit such a small pony.

WHAT DOES IT ACHIEVE?

In order to improve your horse's dexterity and suppleness there are certain things to be aware of when working out a training programme which includes free jumping. Jumps should always be built progressing from easy to more difficult, and each session should include a warm-up phase. It goes without saying that the horse's age, experience and character should also be taken into account. You must be aware that each horse is an individual, and that their capability and experience will vary. The jumps should be set out accordingly, either singly, as a combination or as a grid.

Is it possible to improve rhythm and technique with free jumping? Is it good for flexibility and suppleness? It is of general opinion that neither potential nor established dressage horses should be ridden over very high obstacles, but this is where free jumping can be so useful. Over a small grid or 'in-and-out' the horse can learn to be more supple through the back, be more relaxed and develop impulsion. You have to assess what the horse needs, where the problems lie and what he enjoys. The 'happy hacker' benefits just as much from the gymnastic and fittening work that free jumping can offer as a driving horse, race horse, Western horse or show jumper.

Free jumping can really help both young horses at the start of their training, as well as those a bit further on and at the stage of jumping a course, going cross – country or hunting. Without the weight of a rider it is easier for them to get their balance in unfamiliar situations. Also, the inexperienced can learn how to gauge the height of an obstacle and adjust his stride accordingly. As well as jumping single obstacles, combinations and grids set for correct striding, the horse can also learn not to be intimidated by jumps set at more awkward distances and to adjust his stride accordingly.

From the hip downwards the joints of the hind leg flex and bend. This can be clearly seen even over a small cross-pole.

Over small jumps horses can learn to jump for themselves. Faults can creep in when free jumping in the same way as they can under saddle, but horses learn from their own mistakes when free jumping in a different way than when they are under saddle. The horse's ability to cope with different situations is influenced by the rider or trainer's ability to remain in balance with the horse. One factor of free jumping that should not be under-valued is – and this is not exclusive to event riders – that the horse has to decide a suitable stride and

tempo on his own, and when to take off. The construction of the obstacles is vital for this to work in the horse's favour.

While they are still maturing all young horses learn the same lessons from free jumping and develop to the best of their physical ability, tending to jump as high as they can. This does not apply to horses with jumping blood in their veins that tend to be a bit more economical with their efforts and only jump as high as necessary.

Horses with less aptitude for jumping can still

The hind-quarters take a great deal of weight in a canter pirouette. It is easy to see how free jumping can help to develop this type of work. (Photo: Horses in Media/Frieler)

bascule over a fence, improving their forehand technique and the mechanics of their hindquarters within the limits of their conformation. With free jumping it is possible to practice obstacles that can cause problems in a course – such as water jumps.

Although you can generally improve the horse's self-confidence, 'feel' and enthusiasm for work under saddle, with correct and well carried out free jumping this can all be achieved and more, as well as creating the fun element in the horse's training.

FREE JUMPINGS USE IN ALL DISCIPLINES

For a dressage horse, gymnastic jumping is a very beneficial addition to its work, with or without a rider. It benefits all the joints of the hindquarters, namely the hip, stifle and hock joints. In the higher levels of dressage the muscles of the hindquarters need to extend and contract very efficiently in order to achieve collection, with the hindquarters taking weight while maintaining correct gaits.

Free jumping is very beneficial for improving suppleness in horses that have been driven a lot, as well as adding a different aspect to their work. (Photo: Christiane Slawik)

A grid of cavaletti or small cross poles is quite demanding work and builds these muscles very efficiently.

The benefits for long-distance horses are to loosen the neck and back muscles very well. Above all, free jumping is very useful for getting horses fit again after a break, and conversely when winding down after a season's competition. A combination of free jumping with dressage work in a training programme for long-distance riders is a very effective way of improving suppleness, dexterity, body awareness and balance.

Gaited horses can also benefit from free jumping and are quite often required to jump by their breed fraternity. Generally speaking, the high head carriage expected of these horses can result in tension in the back, neck and hindquarters. This can be altered by introducing free jumping to re-establish suppleness and relaxation.

Interestingly enough, a good bascule over a fence is a clear indication of correct back muscle development. Western horses especially need work to build strong hind-quarters. Grid work improves dexterity and the freedom of the shoulders. Free jumping can help a great deal, particularly when training for 'hunter-hack' classes, and involve riding over a small jump where jumping style is taken into account.

It is very important for driving horses that they remain supple. Free jumping in conjunction with dressage work is the way to achieve this. For this sport, grid work is very good for improving freedom through the shoulder, and increasing the speed of reaction, aspects which are just as important as developing the power of the hind quarters. A grid of small jumps is very effective in improving the horse's way of moving forwards - there is no need to build them too high.

IMPROVING THE HORSE'S WELL-BEING, WHETHER YOUNG OR OLD

It goes without saying that the horse must be healthy in order to work over poles, and have no leg problems. With certain back and neck problems free jumping does not necessarily have to be avoided, but it is important to consult your vet as to whether this type of work is suitable for your horse. For example, rounding the back over small obstacles can be beneficial for horses with kissing spines as it can help to strengthen the back muscles and improve the movement of the horse's spine. Another example is horses with arthritis in the neck vertebrae that are not supposed to work on a contact or to be worked in a bit. Through gymnastic free jumping muscle tone can be maintained or improved in preparation for future ridden work. If a show jumper or eventer has had to have a break in its training due to injury it can be gradually brought back into work without the added weight of the rider. In this instance, it is important to ask your vet for advice. There are some situations where jumping would not be allowed, for example with colic operations. Occasionally it may help to explain to the vet the benefits that free jumping can bring where ridden work is not suitable, especially if the vet is only used to horses being jumped under the saddle.

At what age should a horse start to jump? Breeders often allow young foals to jump with their mothers, which gives the breeder a chance to assess the youngster's jumping ability, and also to take photos to be used when advertising the horses for sale. Free jumping over low obstacles can be used as a 'game' for yearlings but it is important not to do any serious training at this age. It can be used occasionally as long as the youngster is confident. Once the young horse reaches three years of age, free jumping can be used between two and eight times a month.

When is a horse to old to jump any more? An older horse that is starting to jump again after a long break should be introduced to free jumping very gradually. If the horse is used to free jumping and has been worked regularly in this way, there is no reason – providing the horse is fit and well – for it to discontinue to jump, as long as it still enjoys the experience. Free jumping should always be part of the horse's training, whether it is a pony, a native breed, a thoroughbred or a Quarter horse.

Jumps can be made more inviting by filling them either with poles or fillers. If you are using planks, you can invert the jump cups as shown here so that they fall easily if hit by the horse.

WHAT DO YOU NEED?

Once you have decided to free-jump your horse on a regular basis, you should think about what equipment you need, although generally you will only need simple things. You can get by with a green field and minimum jump building material, but you may wish to add to this at a later stage. A simple training plan and basic equipment will be explained in this chapter.

POLES, JUMP STANDS, WINGS

Many livery yards have a set of jumps that can also be used for free jumping. It is important to remember that obstacles should progress from low to high and from simple to more complex. This does mean that you need sufficient building material to hand. A simple jump is one with a clear ground line so the horse can easily judge where to take off. An inexperienced horse will find jumps without a ground line much harder.

Many people are under the impression that a horse can be worried by a jump built with lots of poles or planks. This can happen if the horse is unfamiliar with the type or colour of jump it is faced with. The horse must always be calmly introduced to anything new. A fence that has been filled in with poles is much more 'horse-friendly' than one that has large open gaps. Poles may be heavy to carry and jumps can take a bit of time and effort to build, but it does not pay to cut corners for the sake of a bit of hard work. There is an on-going discussion about which colours to use. Some say not to use any yellow poles, and others are of the opinion that jumps with blue and white or blue poles are knocked down more than any other colour. However, the reason for this has not been clarified.

To understand the colour recognition of an animal, separate colours need to be used. Horses can distinguish between the colours yellow, blue and green. In successful trials, horses will also react to the colour red, although the colour receptors in the eye only respond to blue tones at close range vision, and to green and green/yellow at middle to long range vision. Recent investigations have found that the horse can most clearly tell the difference between the colours blue and yellow. Most four-legged animals see their world in monochrome, and also in two tones.

Generally speaking, brightly coloured poles are easier to see. When free jumping it is also important that the jump can be clearly distinguished from the ground, for example building a jump on grass from green poles makes the obstacle more difficult for the horse. White poles are easy to see whether used in an indoor school with a dark surface, on new wood shavings or light-coloured sand. Using poles of a single colour rather than banded with dark and light colours makes it harder for the horse to judge the size and shape of the obstacle. Red and white poles are often used to mark the sides of a jumping lane because they are easy to see and are recognised by the horse.

The horse's eyes are situated so that it can see movement at long distance easily. However, like us it can focus clearly at close range, but in order to use this field of vision it is necessary for it to lower his head. The horse has a wide range of distance vision to alert itself of approaching danger and to give time to run. This 'flight reflex' is very strong in the horse. The horse's ability to focus on movement can be demonstrated by its reaction to fluttering flags at the edge of an arena. An inexperienced horse will be momentarily distracted from the jumping course by this sudden movement and lose concentration. It is very helpful to bear this in mind, not only when free jumping, but in all aspects of the horse's training.

It is very important to use safety jump cups wherever possible. They should at least be used for the top back rail of an oxer just in case the horse should get a pole caught between its legs.

THE IMPORTANCE OF SAFETY

As a guide for when selecting jump-building material, you should not use poles that are too heavy or jump stands with safety cups. Sloping wings are very useful when free jumping. These can be used as a barrier for the jumping lane, or you could use jump stands with poles.

There is a tape on the market that can also be used for marking out the grid by stretching it taut between the wings or jump stands. On no account should electric tape or baler twine be used in case the horse accidentally touches it. Serious injury can easily be prevented by taking care with the materials used.

Another safety issue is to cover mirrors. If you are jumping outdoors, the horse may be distracted by things going on outside the paddock and take off. You must be aware of the horse's flight instinct, or of playfulness, and be very careful that the horse does not jump out over the fence to join its field mates.

Working indoors or outside

Can you free-jump a horse in an outdoor school or a paddock? Certainly! You must, though, follow a few rules, that have been briefly mentioned previously which also apply in the indoor school.

When free jumping in an enclosed area or in the field, you should not construct obstacles higher than the surrounding fence in case the horse takes it into his head to jump this instead. A suggestion is to build a jumping lane in the middle of the field or outdoor school with 'jumping tape' enclosing it on both sides. This is safer than the horse jumping alongside the fence surrounding the field or arena. It is best if the horse is led into the jumping lane each time to keep him calm.

A novice horse can run around and be just as naughty indoors as well as outside. Unfortunately there are occasions indoors where a horse loses its

Mirrors should be covered up to prevent the horse looking into them or trying to jump into them. This is especially important with stallions or horses you are unfamiliar with. A roller blind, as shown here, is ideal.

head though panic and stress, and jumps either out of the arena or into the viewing gallery. It is therefore very important to keep the horse calm at all times.

Over-reach boots and tendon boots are useful, as shown here. The tendon boots protect the back of the tendons and fetlocks from injury by the hind feet, while the over-reach boots help to prevent the shoe from being pulled off.

Protective equipment for the horse

For free jumping the forelegs should be protected by bandages or boots, and hind legs with fetlock boots. Your choice of protection will depend upon the individual horse. If the horse catches its front legs or the heels of the front feet, then appropriate boots should be used. For basic protection, either neoprene boots with a padded area over the inside of the fetlock, or leather boots can be used. There is a point of view that an unshod horse can jump without boots, but there is always the risk that the horse will hit a pole, or catch a leg should it play around. Naturally, an unprotected horse stands a greater chance of becoming injured, especially if it catches itself on its front heels. If the horse is shod in front, then over-reach boots are a good idea to prevent it from catching a shoe. If horses catch their fetlocks behind then fetlock boots can be used.

You can jump your horse with either a bridle or head collar. Horses that need to be led into jumps frequently are better in a bridle. Also, young horses that are just getting used to wearing a bit can be jumped in a bridle. This is a good way to gently accustom them to wearing a bridle, but you should not introduce both new things at once.

The lead-rein should be about 80 cm long, and with no knots or clips on the ends so that it can run freely through the bit or head collar rings. It works best if you have a long and short end in your hand. You let go of the short end shortly before the jump, before the horse takes over himself. Let him go at the beginning of the jumping lane. With a very inexperienced horse you may need to lead him in hand over ground poles or small jumps, in which case use a longer, thick rope which is easier to keep hold of than a thin short one. With a short rope, you put yourself in a dangerous position by being too close to the horse should he jump in an uncontrolled manner. It is important that the horse has respect for his leader when being led by a person. This can be achieved by work in-hand.

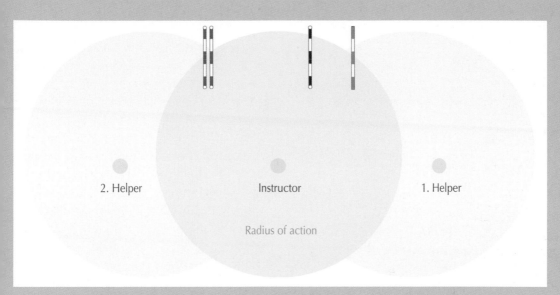

The team of three helpers work together either in the indoor or outdoor school. The most experienced person is best positioned by the jumps.

PROFICIENT HELPERS

For classical free jumping one builds a grid on the long side of the school, preferably going away from the entrance and with a team of three helpers. The first stands by the entrance to the jumping lane, the second level with the middle of the grid, and the third after the last jump. Each individual must be careful with their body language, so they do not inadvertently turn the horse around. Utmost concentration is needed to 'pass' the horse onwards to the next helper. It is best that the person level with the middle of the grid has a whip with a short lash, such as a driving whip. The other two helpers need to be equipped with lunge whips. In a 20 by 40 metre arena, the jumps should be placed so that there is at least 15 metres after the last jump, allowing plenty of room before the horse reaches the corner.

Having three helpers is the ideal scenario, and it does not matter whether the horse is stopped after each jump or continues a few times around. If you are alone, it is best to build a short grid, such as an in out so that the horse does not build up to much power. Once the horse understands what free jumping is all about, and enjoys it, then you can introduce a longer grid, or even a continuous jumping lane around the whole school. (See chapter 'Jump Building Suggestions' page 55.)

Three metre long poles are ideal, four metre poles are also suitable, but can be rather heavy to carry. They create a wider grid, where you run the risk of the horse turning around. Poles should be placed on an angle at the side of the first jump and after the last to encourage the horse to jump straight. This gives the horse confidence on the approach, and also helps him to remain straight after the last jump. These poles should be raised one and a half to two metres off the ground so that the horse acknowledges them. Raised poles can also be placed a couple of metres from the track in the corners, reducing the risk of the horse turning around and making it easier to keep him going in one direction around the school.

When free jumping, plastic cones are useful for keeping the horse on a straight course through the grid.

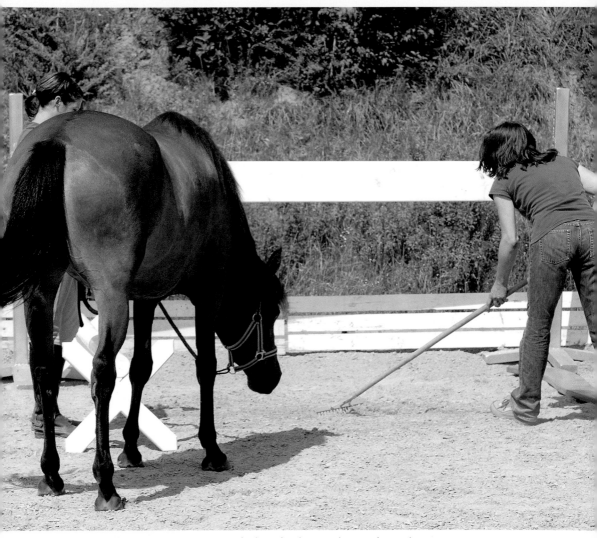

If there are a lot of horses free jumping it is important to rake the surface between the jumps frequently. The whole school must be properly levelled after the session.

ORGANISING THE TRAINING SESSION

If free jumping is not done at your stables then ask permission and get a few horse owners together to plan a training session, dividing the building and dismantling of jumps and the training work between you. If you have a lot of horses to work then choose a rest day at the stable yard when the school is not busy. Organise this with the yard owner, or maybe hire a freelance trainer to help.

If you are working on your own, or it is not possible to use the whole arena for free jumping, section off part of the school with jump stands and poles or 'jumping tape' to free-jump your horse in. Alternatively you could jump your horse in an outdoor school or in a field, keeping him on a lunge rein or long rope. This works well over one or two jumps.

Light and weatherproof – that is the advantage of aluminium jump stands.

Costs involved

When free jumping, the obstacles need to be very inviting and need more jump-building material than normal jump training. With just two or three jumps built from stands, poles and fillers, you are already looking at a cost of a hundred pounds or so. If your stable yard has no jumps, consider buying some. If the yard owner is willing, offer to make a contribution towards the cost of some jumps and the cost of levelling the arena surface afterwards. This can result in a more manageable cost. When free jump-

ing is carried out by several riders, with a willing riding instructor the cost can be reduced further, depending on the number of horses. An inexpensive way of acquiring jump material is from show organisers, who may sell old jumps quite cheaply, which are quite suitable for training purposes.

Or you could buy timber from a woodyard and make some yourself. Whether you choose wooden or aluminium jump stands depends on the price and ease of use. Aluminium stands do not rot and are lighter to move around, but are usually more expensive than wood.

What about plastic jumps?

If high obstacles are not required, plastic blocks can be used. There are different shapes of block that can be used to build jumps up to 1.10 metres high, and also to build small spreads.

This type of jump works especially well for young horses, or when jumping is used for loosening up. There are many types of jump that can be used as cavaletti, oxers or uprights. Plastic poles are also available. These are weather-resistant and, as with plastic blocks, can be left outside as opposed to wooden ones which should be protected from the wet in case they rot. Some types of block are designed so that the poles do not fall if the horse should hit them, but this can be dangerous. Jumps should always be built so that the poles can roll off – this being the advantage of using conventional jump stands. Also the height of the obstacles can be more varied when using jump stands as opposed to blocks. Cavaletti made from synthetic material are lighter to carry than wooden ones, and have greater height variation.

LET'S GET GOING

While the jumps are being built for the first horse, you should already be preparing for the free jumping session. How you warm your horse up is up to you and depends on the horse, the facilities, and the number of helpers available. It is vital for your horse's health and well-being to at least give him a basic warm up beforehand.

Taking the horse for a short walk in hand is an ideal warm up.

WARMING UP

You could walk your horse calmly outside in the fresh air, allowing it to have a change of scenery. This option can be preferable to allowing the horse to 'let off steam' on the lunge where he may buck and tear around, which will not do him a lot of good. Walking exercise is the most beneficial for the muscles, tendons and ligaments and joints to function properly. You often hear that if the horse has just been brought in from the field or an open stall that he does not need to be warmed up: this is not true. Firstly the horse is not compelled to move about sufficiently to loosen his body, besides which, moving a few steps to the left and back again, does not constitute a warm up.

A good way of warming up is to lunge the horse over ground poles.

Walking is important

A short walk is not sufficient as a warm up for stabled horses in the middle of winter. They should walk for at least fifteen minutes; less than ten minutes is not enough – even in summer. Without looking at the time, you could easily underestimate how long you have walked your horse for.

What you think is ten minutes may actually only turn out to be five. Many riders have discovered that walking the horse in hand is an enjoyable experience, and it helps to develop a closer relationship between them.

Naturally, you could begin by warming your horse up on a horse-walker. This can be followed by lunge work in trot, which for this purpose can be done in a head collar. Alternatively, if you are using free jumping as gymnastic work to loosen the back, you could prepare the horse by lungeing him in side reins or over ground poles in the warm up.

On the other hand, warming up on the lunge at a distance from the jumps has the advantage of giving you more control over the horse. If you allow the horse to warm up free around the school, you must be careful that he does not jump the obstacles prematurely, or that he stops suddenly, or turns sharply on his haunches.

It is best to warm up on the lunge in trot in another school, right away from the obstacles. If there are enough helpers, then the horse can be worked free between them and kept away from the jumps.

Once the horse is familiar with both ground work and leading in-hand then the horse can be led over the first small jump.

TIPS ON HOW TO BEGIN

With a young or inexperienced horse, you should begin with one pole on the ground. When the horse is supple and relaxed on both reins in trot and canter you could then introduce a small upright jump at a maximum height of 50 centimetres which is to be jumped on both reins. Next, you can lead the horse on a rope over poles on the ground, again in walk and trot. Sometimes it works well to place a pole before the upright jump at a distance of either 5.5 metres or 2.5 metres. It is most important to keep the jump small so the horse can calmly work it out for himself. It is also important that the horse is confident before you progress to the next stage. When a young horse is unsettled by the unfamiliar surroundings of an indoor school he should just

be quietly worked over ground poles until he is settled. There will only be a small amount of the work that you will be satisfied with the first time. You have to ask yourself whether the training session was successful or not, or whether there will be improvement in the future. You can familiarise the young horse with the jumping lane by letting him go through it first of all without any jumps set up. This is also useful for a tense horse so that he can learn to relax.

Horses are flight animals and have their eyes positioned on the sides of their heads for good all-round vision. When young horses start their free jumping training they learn to concentrate on the obstacle in front of them rather than looking be-

Get to know your horse. If you are the whip-handler, it is very important that you have the horse's trust from the beginning.

hind and to the sides. It becomes apparent how difficult this is when a young horse is asked to go over a pole for the first time. The horse may trip many times because it is looking all over the place and not at the pole. Groundwork teaches the horse to look where it is going. In-hand work over a single pole to start with, then several poles, helps to develop this ability. The same method can be used should you have an older horse that is unfamiliar with free jumping or working over coloured poles.

How does the horse learn?

It is very important to know how the horse learns from different situations. When free jumping, it is often said that the horse learns from every experience, even in the situation of a fall, as long as it is correctly dealt with at the time. If not handled correctly, the horse's progress can be held back in such a case. The horse works out for itself how to use its back when free jumping.

Learning means when a new experience is assimilated or an old skill is improved and built upon. The basis for learning is the use of relevant exercises. With expensive animals, learning is based upon three rules: the first is prevention of bad experiences and encouraging good ones, the second is developing a new habit and the third is imitating others. The third option does not come into free jumping, especially in an enclosed indoor school. If free jumping is done outside, or in a school with a view through the windows, or in a field or paddock, then horses can learn from each other – both good and bad things.

What you do not want is a horse that comes incorrectly into an obstacle; the approach is hesitant and un-rhythmical rather than fluid, or the horse hurts itself by hitting a pole; the horse either rushes forwards when landing or conversely cannot canter fluently after the jump.

Why is this so? As a flight animal, the horse has a good sense of self-preservation and will keep itself fit, well and out of trouble as best it can. This behaviour is inherited rather than learned. It is possible that predatory animals are not really aware of any pain or discomfort they may be in when they are hunting their prey. Horses are world champions at compensating for pain without losing quality of movement. They have a genetic and practical ability to ensure that the approach and take-off at a jump is harmonious and round. This could also explain why a horse generally tries to jump better each time, and improves as it learns from each situation.

If the jump construction is too difficult for the horse it will still try to cope, but it may learn that free jumping is difficult and can cause pain. After such an incident it would be sensible to make the exercise easier so the horse gets its confidence back as soon as possible. This also minimises the risk of injury.

The wrong way to do it

A trainer, and every person who is around horses, should be able to tell the difference between what is right and what is wrong for the horse and they must be aware of the horse's reactions.

Usually you can utilise both praise and punishment during daily contact with the horse. When free jumping one can learn how important it is to give praise for good work. You can get the horse to understand what is required by using the voice and whip aids. From an animal welfare point of view, strong demands should not be placed upon the horse. However, problems can arise when the whip aids are given too strongly on the approach, driving the horse into an obstacle that it is not experienced enough for.

Driving the horse too fast into the obstacles can be counter-productive, and you will not achieve the result you expect. The horse will jump 'flat' with a tight back and learn to rush at jumps. (See chapter 'Improving Attitude Fault Correction' page 66) Horses that are going too fast are likely to run into the walls and injure themselves.

Calmness is important during every attempt. If the horse is not one hundred percent confident about what he is doing, you can help him by leading him in hand in trot.

Making free jumping fun

When free jumping, you can praise the horse with your voice and give him a reward after the grid. This has the advantage of giving the horse a short rest and a quiet moment after jumping, so he learns to remain relaxed. This is the way for free jumping to be enjoyable, and with enjoyment comes the development of trust and improvement of self-confidence with every successful training session. It is not only show jumping riders who need the horse to cope with unfamiliar situations and to learn from its mistakes. The benefits of this training are not just superficial: anyone who works a horse with sensitivity and who concentrates on every detail will be able to train using subtle voice and whip aids. When free jumping, horses can learn without the disturbance of a rider, thereby avoiding, for example, a wrongly applied heel aid or a sharp rein aid. This can happen to the best of riders during a poor jumping round. A novice horse will be inconsistent in the way it jumps – even when free jumping – and such an experience can be stressful. A bad experience can affect the way the horse jumps the next time, so it is important to deal with each situation carefully.

Relaxed and attentive, this gelding trots confidently after the jumping grid.

The first training session

The requirements of free jumping are dependent upon the horse – that is to take into account the horse's experience, age, constitution, condition and strength. Basically this means an experienced horse after just a short warm up is capable of jumping one or two small jumps proficiently.

High, wide jumps, long grids and bigger distances belong at the end of the session for the experienced horse. This does, however, depend on the horse's physical strength. With a young and inexperienced, or an untrained horse, it is sensible to halt the horse before every attempt.

This gives it a chance to catch its breath and to calm down. During the pause, the team of helpers can change or raise the jumps as necessary, rather than letting the horse run again and again over the same grid, as is so often witnessed.

Praise is important – also when free jumping. A friendly word and a treat are just as important as having a break after jumping a grid.

Why work on the left rein?

Horses, as with all living creatures, are either right- or left-handed. Approximately 90 percent of humans are right-handed and the rest are left-handed. This has been so throughout history and records of this can be seen in pictures and sculptures from Prehistoric times. What is interesting is how a right-hander turns to the left – whether human or equine – when they are moving freely.

When travelling over unfamiliar territory in a left-handed direction people, as well as horses and other animals, take several hours longer to get back to the starting point. With horses, right-handedness has other applications: Right-handed horses favour left lead canter. In left canter, the right foreleg carries the least weight. In the moment when two legs are on the ground, the weight of the heavy forehand, plus eventually the rider's weight, is propelled forwards and upwards. Nearly all horses free-jump better on the left rein, even right-handed horses jump more purposefully.

However, it can be worthwhile to work on the other rein for a short time (see chapter 'Jump Building Suggestions' page 52). But take care: a horse must not just continually work in one direction because of being left-or right-handed. The horse sees a different picture with its right eye than its left. Changing direction presents a different picture and situation to the horse each time. For example, when hacking out, if a rubbish bin is always on the right hand side and it is suddenly moved to the left, this creates a problem for the horse. The understanding of this today is that it is caused by the lack of communication between both sides of the brain.

How often should you train?

In the beginning, free jumping can be quietly introduced twice a week. A regular weekly session is ideal, but it is not a problem if young horses are free-jumped less frequently than this. The question is always: what will be achieved? When a young horse is being trained it needs to take everything in at its own pace. Jumping once a month can be a part of the learning process and help the horse to get used to being handled by people. The most important thing is that training is carried out on a regular basis.

TIPS FOR THE TRAINING SESSION

Once the horse has become accustomed to the training system and enjoys free jumping it is important to add variety. Mistakes and injuries can be caused by carelessness. Should the horse become inattentive, then the number of obstacles can be increased, an in-and-out grid can be introduced or you could lay ground poles in between the jumps to improve the horse's concentration.

Another alternative is to vary the type of obstacle used. (See chapter 'Jump Building Suggestions' page 52). Now and again, single jumps can be raised. It is important, however, to not allow the horse to become bored and to have a regard for the technical aspects when introducing something new. Care must be taken not only for the horse's legs and physical well – being, but for developing its confidence and ability to cope with new situations.

How to know when to stop

After a few warm-up jumps, going over the grid five or six times is enough. The jumps can be gradually raised, or the distances increased during this time until the final height and jump spacing is reached. If the grid is totally new to the horse then one successful run through is sufficient for that day.

To prevent injury it is important to finish on a good note before the horse becomes tired and starts to make mistakes. If you have been too ambitious and built jumps whose difficulty is too great for the horse, then it is important to lower the jumps and make the grid easier. It is better still not to get into this situation. If the horse is breathing heavily and is tense after a training session then you must review the whole training programme for the horse.

Using the lunge whip

Understanding the correct use of the lunge whip is just as important for the whip – handler as it is for the horse. If the horse is used to work on the lunge and is familiar with the lunge whip, there should normally be no problem.

With free jumping the horse has to cope with three people, each with a whip in their hand, so it is sensible to organise the helpers as follows.

The most important person is in the middle and can crack the whip to encourage the horse as necessary. Each of the other two helpers should hold the whip with an outstretched arm, and move about accordingly to guide the horse around the school. What applies when lungeing is also relevant here – using the lunge whip towards the hock joint drives the horse forwards, and towards the shoulder or girth keeps the horse out and discourages it from falling in towards the trainer. Just before the jump the chief whip-handler can drive the horse forwards either by cracking the whip or by sweeping the whip towards the horse from behind. With an experienced whip-handler a light touch on the hind cannon bone directly before the jump can ask the horse to step more under its centre of gravity on take-off. In this situation less is definitely more – next time the aids should be smaller as the horse learns what is required. The whip has done its job, and becomes superficial, once the horse has learnt to react just to the voice aid.

JUMPING ON THE LUNGE

You can also jump the horse on the lunge or double-lunge (long reins). The latter is best carried out if you are already experienced with using this particular form of training. A horse can be trained to free-jump perfectly well on a single lunge line using a reduced grid. It is important that the horse is first used to being worked on the lunge. You can lunge the horse either from a head collar or a lunge cavesson.

There may be situations where you wish to lunge from the bridle, but if you are inexperienced you must be careful not to accidentally pull the horse

This gelding is familiar with jumping on the lunge. It would be even better without the slight pull to the side with the lunge line that you can see in this photo.

suddenly in the mouth when it jumps. You should only jump a quiet, trained horse on the lunge from the bridle. The greatest risk when jumping on the lunge is getting the lunge line caught up on an obstacle. In this situation, it is advisable to use plastic blocks or short jump wings with guide poles laid on them so that the lunge line can slide over them. On the lunge you should use smaller jumps than with free jumping at a maximum of 80 cm. The horse is only on a straight line for a moment when working on a circle. For this reason, the circle must be a minimum of 20 metres in diameter.

Ideally the horse should jump from trot on the lunge as this is best for developing muscle, improving self-confidence, and keeping calm. Also it is better for the horse's legs. It is best if the horse is allowed to go out on the lunge line just before the jump so it has as much room as possible to come in on a straight line. It is important not to pull or to hang on to the lunge line during the take-off and over the jump as this will disturb the horse. If the horse copes well with a single fence you could introduce jumps on a circle at a later stage. Another alternative is to build an oxer or upright fence on the closed side of the circle, and three or four trotting poles on the open side.

Alternatively, you place trotting poles nearer to the jump to make sure the horse jumps from trot, which develops more impulsion. The lowest jumps should be placed on the open side of the circle and should have wings on the outside to prevent the horse running out, particularly if the horse is young and needs security. This also applies if you are jumping in an outdoor school. This can be constructed from wings or jump stands with jumping tape between them.

DEVELOPING AN EYE FOR CORRECT TRAININ

What should you be aware of? It is important to develop your powers of observation.
The better you can interpret what you see – and this applies in daily life as well as when training
horses – the better you will understand your horse and how it reacts to different situations.

WHAT TO LOOK FOR

It is best to develop your own perception with a simple grid that the horse is familiar with. You can assess how a horse jumps naturally over a low jump without any ground poles before it.

Are the canter strides all the same?

Did the horse take off where it should do or was it too far away/too close to the jump?

It is important not to stand too close to the jump or you will not be able to see clearly how the horse approaches and how it copes with the jump. If you have natural talent, you will be able to see if a horse is going to take off at the right place six or seven strides before an obstacle, even if you have never seen a horse jump before. Others must learn to be able to do this.

What is the difference between a positive attitude and jumping stress? When is the horse mentally attuned to the job in hand? The demands placed on each animal must be suitable for the needs of the individual. In order for the horse to develop in the right way it is important for you to train you eye and your own powers of observation. It helps to know what is special for each horse and what their normal way of going is beforehand.

For this reason it is best to follow these criteria in the following order:

- How does the horse jump – is it supple or stiff?
- How does the horse move towards the jump – is it relaxed or tense?
- What is the tempo? Does the horse go faster or slower towards the jump?
- Does the horse concentrate on the situation or is its mind elsewhere?
- Is the take-off good? Does the horse get too close to the jump if there is no ground line? Does it take off too far away?
- Does it bascule over the fence, or jump with a hollow back?
- How is the front leg technique? Does the horse leave them hanging from the elbow or knee or does it bend both joints to jump cleanly?
- How is the hind leg technique? Does the horse jump with its hind legs out behind or does it tuck them up under the stomach?
- How fluent and flexible is the landing and how fluently does the horse canter on afterwards?

Here the foam padding under the jump is dual purpose – not only does it define the ground line, it also encourages the horse to jump with more effort and improves the bascule.

1 *Point of shoulder*

2 *Elbow*

3 *Forearm*

4 *Knee*

5 *Cannon bone*

6 *Hock*

7 *Thigh*

8 *Stifle*

9 *Hip joint*

10 *Point of hip*

It is beneficial to watch free jumping done by a professional trainer a few times. You can also pick up useful information by watching different classes at a show jumping competition. Find an obstacle that you can see clearly from the side and where you can concentrate without being disturbed. Watch a number of horses over the same jump and then do the same with a totally different one. Start with a novice class and see what a different picture you get compared with professional riders at top level. Another option is to watch show jumping on television, video or DVD. It can be useful if you have the facility to repeat a particular moment on the film and watch the same jump several times over. Watching as much as you can helps you to understand your own horse and to train your eye. Private films can be found on the internet showing both good and bad attempts at jumping. The more horses you observe the better understanding you will have about how each individual horse copes with jumping. The following examples should help you to recognise and deal with different faults and problems that you could encounter.

In order to show as much information as possible in the photos in this book they may show details that are different from the text. For example, the barrier before the jump may be left out to give a better view of the horse in action. Similarly, if a cross pole is used it is harder to judge whether the jump is substantial enough. The following text has been set out to give as much detail as possible, but it is not necessarily what would be recommended in normal training.

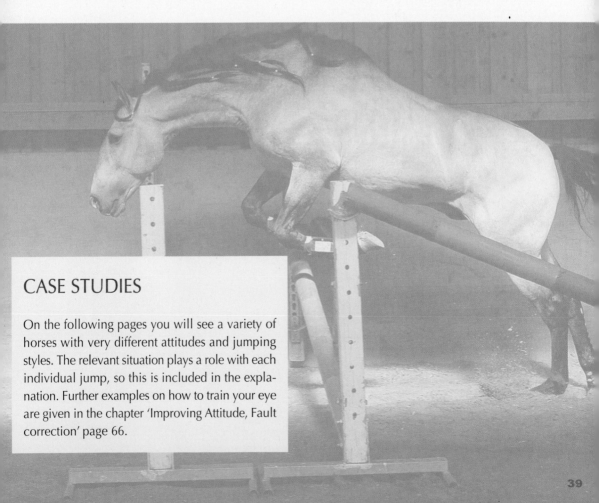

CASE STUDIES

On the following pages you will see a variety of horses with very different attitudes and jumping styles. The relevant situation plays a role with each individual jump, so this is included in the explanation. Further examples on how to train your eye are given in the chapter 'Improving Attitude, Fault correction' page 66.

Nellaun, a 17-year-old Haflinger stallion is a seasoned free-jumper. He finds a brisk canter tempo and jumps totally for himself.

You dare not chase him forwards otherwise he becomes too keen and no longer finds the correct point of take-off.

Here you can see that he is already rounding his back before the jump (1), and jumps with his hind legs well under his centre of gravity (2 & 3). He finds the correct take-off point and jumps with a good shape over the jump. The forearm is lifted up correctly and the knee is extremely flexed (3). In the downward phase of the jump the hind quarters clearly open away (5).

He jumps a bit too high, but this just shows his exuberance. As a result he only requires minimal fillers in the fences (3). He flies over the jump (4) – this small oxer is no problem for him at all.

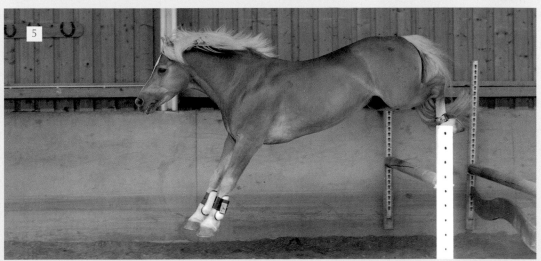

This 13-year-old Bayern Warmblood has jumping blood from his Holstein father. His mother is a trotter.

He has a lot of jumping ability and a good attitude but does not jump regularly, hence he tends to jump too high.

Here you can see that when he goes over the jump his forelegs are not flexed very well at the knee (3). As a result of his inexperience he tends to give the jumps too much room at present (4). Otherwise he jumps well, although he can take off a bit too early (2) and must be careful that he does not make a mistake with his hind legs (5). In order that he does not get into difficulty he needs to learn to jump with both hind legs raised the same.

If he leaves a leg trailing he could knock the jump and injure himself (2). He does not jump in an ideal way but is supple and elastic and you can see that he can open his hindquarters well (6).

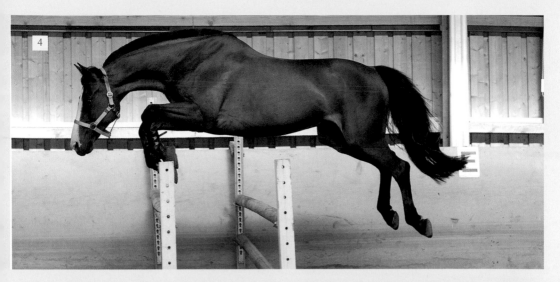

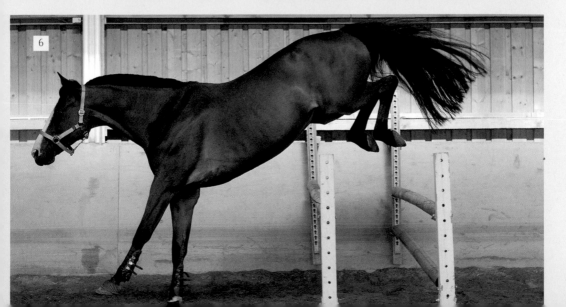

The 6-year-old Lusitano stallion, Util, is a real powerhouse, and has had two years dressage training under saddle and on the double lunge.

He is familiar with free jumping but has not had an established training routine. He comes into the jump very fast – with the wind under his tail – but jumps with his hind legs well under his centre of gravity (1). He comes off the ground at speed, and as a result of his inexperience, takes off far too early (2) and must then jump at full stretch (3). For this reason the bascule over the jump is not ideal and he does not use his back well (4).

While he does tuck his forelegs up very well (3), he tightens and hollows his back when he lands (5) and comes onto his forehand on landing, before cantering on in balance afterwards.

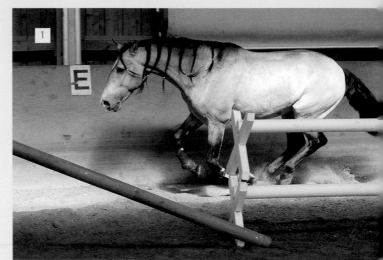

The 5-year-old Lusitano stallion, Faro, is descended from one of the best Portugese bull-fighting breeding lines. He has already jumped out of his paddock from a stand still over a 1.5 metres high fence, but he has barely any experience in free jumping.

Before the jump he is already round (1), but just before the jump he appears to be irritated. This is the first time he has come so close up to a jump, but the take-off point is actually ideal. On the previous two attempts he took off too early. He comes into the jump relatively lack-lustre, with his forelegs hanging and without lifting his back (3). The hind legs are also trailing and he promptly touches a pole (5). He lifts his head high on landing in order to regain his balance after this distraction (6). His foreleg technique improved with a few more attempts.

This 8-year-old branded Bayern mare, Tessina, has a Shagya Arab for a father. She is trained for dressage and free-jumps regularly.

Here you can see that the mare tenses up and does not move freely. In spite of this, she has actually developed a very good technique during training and has come to an ideal take-off point – although you can see she has lost some fluency of movement. She hesitates here with a tightened back (2) and even jumps to one side (3) over this small oxer. It seems an eternity before she actually leaves the ground (4) as her forelegs do not lift quickly enough in front, and after the landing she does not canter forwards fluently. The reason for this with this sensitive mare is her resentment at having to jump in this direction.

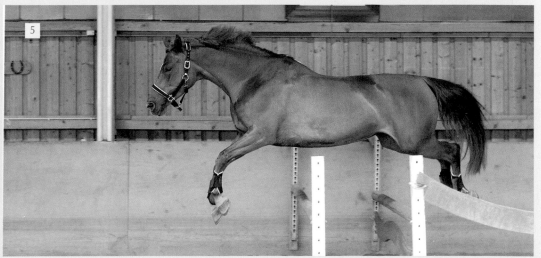

This Shetland pony, Jack, is 15-years-old, regularly ridden, and jumped with and without a rider. This gelding is familiar with free jumping.

He is fundamentally a right-hander, comes in to the jump on the right canter lead, but changes leg directly before the jump (1 & 2) and lands in left lead canter, which he then maintains. His front leg technique is exceptional (3). Also you can see that a cross-pole for a small pony is much more of a challenge that it is for a big horse. Jack takes off a bit early (3) but flies easily over the jump with not even a millimetre to spare (4).

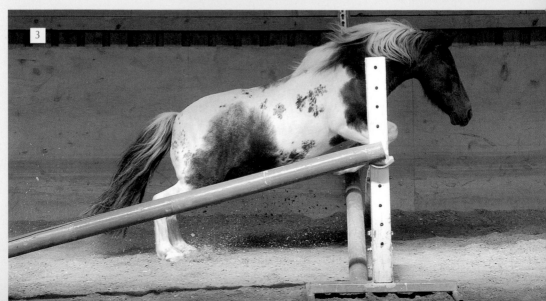

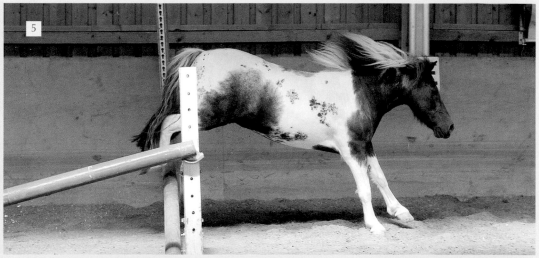

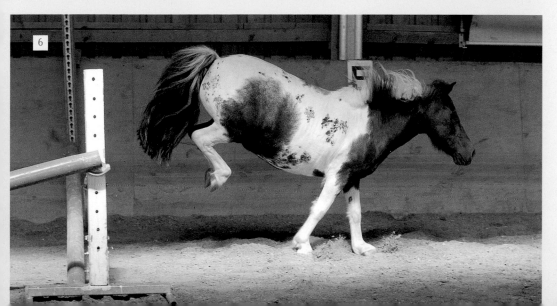

JUMP BUILDING SUGGESTIONS

DISTANCES BETWEEN OBSTACLES

In general, you should allow 3 metres for the canter stride of a big horse, but this does depend on the individual. A canter stride can be anything from less than 3 metres to over 4 metres depending on the ground cover and tempo. For take-off and landing allow half a canter stride for each. With a row of ground poles, cavaletti or raised poles, allow the same as for an in-and-out, i.e, 3 metres.

For one non-jumping stride between the two elements of a double, allow a minimum of 6 metres. If the jumps are high and wide, or with a raised back pole (ascending spread), then allow 8 metres for the non-jumping stride. The higher the jump, the greater the distance should be so as not to hinder the shape the horse makes over the jump. After jumping big, which the horse can do even over a small obstacle, the horse will land further away from it. The higher the jump, the bigger the canter strides are afterwards.

If you have more than one non-jumping stride between obstacles, then a further 3.50 metres should be allowed for each additional canter stride. If you have three strides or more between jumps this would be described as a related distance rather than a combination.

When free jumping, combination fences are used as opposed to related distances. The distance for trotting poles varies more than with canter exercises, and can be set from 1.20 metres to 1.50 metres apart. This is even less with small ponies.

Distances between obstacles

Trot poles .... 1.20 to 1.50 metres
In-out .... about 3 metres
Combination with one-jumping stride
about 7 metres
Combination with two non-jumping strides
about 10 metres

A word of warning:
The length of the horse's canter stride may not conform to these distances. Ideally you should measure your horse's canter stride for accuracy. (See page 54.)

With a small upright fence 1.20 metres high, the ground line should be about 60 cm before the jump. Distances for an average horse (about 16 hands high).

MAKING THE OBSTACLES INVITING

When jumpbuilding, it is important to make the obstacles friendly and inviting. This means that you should fill the space under the jumps with sufficient planks, cross-poles, gates or fillers. A jump with an empty space underneath is much harder for the horse and it will often not take the jump boldly enough, which can be dangerous. It is important to use a ground line as a jump is much more difficult without one. Depending on the height and type of jump the ground line should be about 80 cm before the obstacle to give the horse a clear take-off point. An upright fence is more difficult for the horse than a spread, and makes the take-off easier. When free jumping over an oxer the rear pole should be raised so that it is clearly visible. If you are building jumps for the first time, or you are unsure about size and distance, it is important to use a tape measure.

You should at least get to know how long a metre is when setting out distances. Stride this out with your own steps – you will need to do this anyway when you are jumping under saddle so you can work out the striding between fences. You can mark out where to place the jump stands on the ground by making grooves in the sand, or in the field, with the heel of your boot. Get to know what a 3 metre distance looks like, and you can go on from there.

Measuring or guesswork?

The measurements given are for a typical warmblood with a canter stride of three metres in length. This can vary a lot, depending on the tempo of the horse's gait. Coming in to a grid in trot means the initial stride will be about 20 cm shorter.

It is important to know the type of canter stride the horse has as even the fact that you are jumping the horse on the left rein can have an effect. The aim is to keep the amount of measuring you do to a minimum.

How does my horse canter?

It is helpful and interesting to know how to measure your horse's stride, whether you have a big or small animal. Ride in working canter on the long side and then repeat with a shorter, then a longer stride. The hoof prints are best seen on a flat part of the surface on the inside of the track. You should take a moment to identify when the horse comes off the ground during the canter stride.

The canter stride begins with one hind leg after the period of suspension. In left canter, it is the right hind leg. The second phase is three legs on the ground, i.e. all legs except the left foreleg.

The horse comes off the ground between the first and second phases. The better the horse steps under its centre of gravity after the period of suspension, the more powerfully and cleanly it can come off the ground. The stride measurement should be taken from the print of the outside hind foot.

EXAMPLES FOR ALL SITUATIONS

Ultimately how you select the type of jump and the distance between obstacles depends on how well you know your horse. Narrow distances between the fences will shorten the horse's stride. Wider distances and high, wide jumps, such as an oxer or triple bar, will encourage the horse to stretch and jump more boldly.

In-outs improve speed of reaction and flexibility. It is important to take care not to suddenly raise the height and number of obstacles from that which the horse is accustomed to. During the warm-up phase and when starting out jumps should not exceed 80 cm in height. Talented horses and those with more experience can progress to 1.20 m in height, or even more in exceptional circumstances. Free jumping is very useful for introducing the horse to new situations or objects.

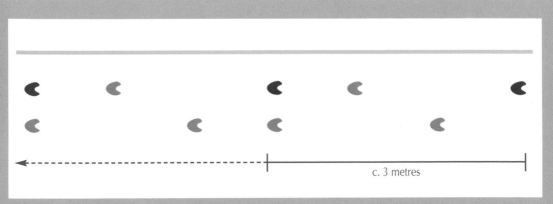

Two canter strides in left lead canter: right hind (shown in dark brown) starts. In working canter, after the period of suspension, the right hind foot steps in the print left by the left fore.

c. 3 metres

A couple of rugs or a tarpaulin that is not too light can be use to simulate a wall by hanging them over a small oxer due to them making the jump much more imposing.

You can build natural jumps using brush fillers or you could simulate a water jump with a blue tarpaulin firstly underneath a cavaletti, and later under a small oxer. You could also hang rugs or material over the poles for even greater variety; the options are endless. It is important to introduce anything new gradually so you do not lose the horse's trust or confidence, and to always remain cool, calm and collected yourself. Hose pipes can have a dual purpose – when free jumping they can be used as a safe alternative to ground poles between the jumps or as trotting poles leading into a grid.

A tarpaulin used to simulate a water jump.
As shown here, always start off small. Allow the horse to familiarise itself with anything new so it remains calm and confident.

Here is an overview of the materials used.

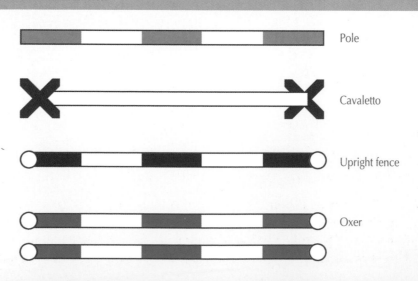

Pole

Cavaletto

Upright fence

Oxer

Starting out

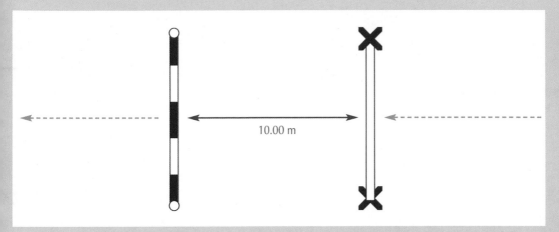

Example 1:

The first jump is a cavaletti followed by two canter strides to give the horse time to shorten or lengthen in preparation for the small upright which should be between 50–80 cm high. There is the option to make the upright, at a maximum height of 80 cm, into a small oxer, no more than 40 cm wide, with the back rail raised for good visibility.

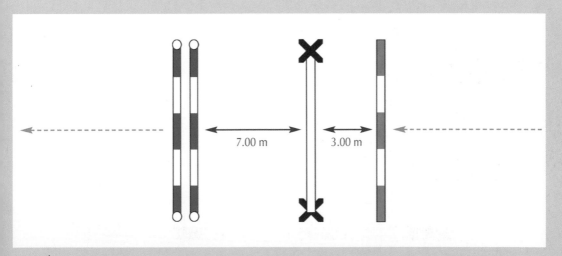

Example 2:

Here a pole is the first element. It is best if the horse begins to trot just before the pole. The cavaletti can later be used as a small upright jump. In the beginning the oxer should be no more than 80 cm high and 40 cm wide. If the jumps are raised to more than a metre in height then the distance between the upright and oxer should be increased accordingly.

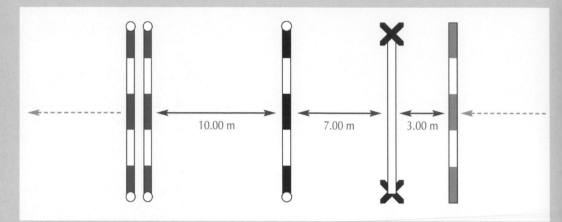

Example 3:
This is basically the 'beginner's version' of a grid. Using the ground pole to bring the horse to the cavaletti correctly also sets the horse up for the upright. Should the horse jump 'big' over the upright, the two non-jumping strides before the oxer allow it to regulate its stride without disturbing the fluency of the canter. This is a good exercise for developing rhythm and dexterity.
Most horses will be able to cope with this grid – built at a maximum heigher of 80 cm – after a few attempts.

Further examples

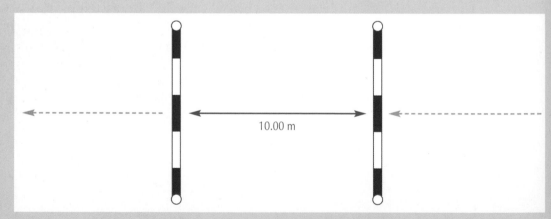

Example 4:
Two inviting upright fences are normally no problem for a horse. The distance between them may need to be increased by half a metre depending on factors such as the length of the canter stride, the speed of the horse, and whether the horse is jumping towards the exit.
Over an upright you can assess the horse's skill, quality and carefulness, particularly with minimum use of wings. Flexibility and bascule can also be observed.

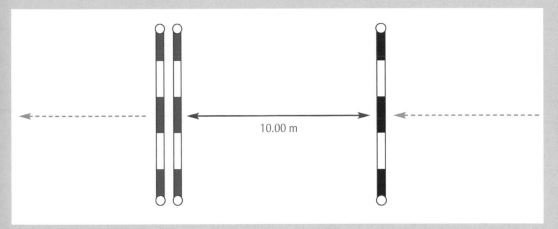

10.00 m

Example 5:
A high jump can be made easier by laying the ground line about 60 cm in front of it.
A ground pole three metres before the jump can be added at a later stage to give an accurate take-off in this double. If you use the obstacles in the other direction, jumping the oxer first, the distance should be slightly decreased. If the upright and oxer are at the end of a grid, then it is important to increase the distance.

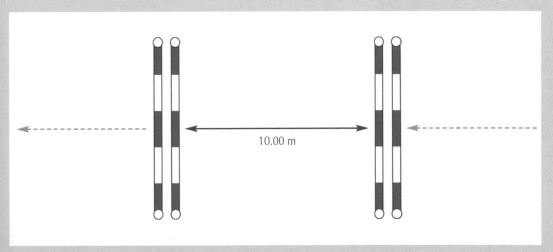

10.00 m

Example 6:
The horse should already be experienced and have developed sufficient skill to jump a double of two oxers. When introducing this exercise it can be made easier by keeping the jumps low and the distance between them shorter. There are several reasons for this: the second half of the jumping arc is both steeper and shorter over an oxer. The ideal landing point after an oxer is the same as for an upright, and this is also the point when impulsion can be lost.

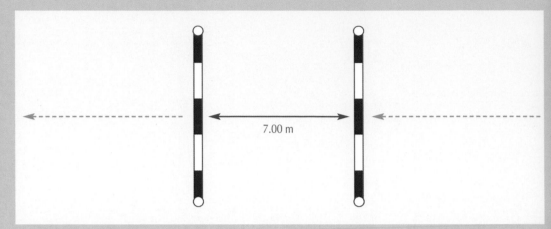

Example 7:
A combination with only one non-jumping stride increases the horse's flexibility as it has to decide quickly whether it jumps too big or too small over the first element. The horse should be encouraged with voice aids to calm it down or to drive it forwards. With more experienced horses, using a narrow distance improves the fore leg technique. In this way careless horses can learn to pay more attention to the job in hand. It is, however, important to shorten the distance gradually.
The double can be jumped in both directions if a ground line is not used, or you could place one each side of both obstacles.

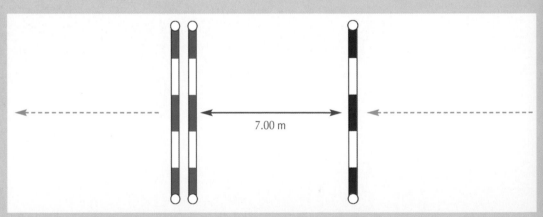

Example 8:
When the obstacles are higher than the horse is used to, it can help to place a ground pole 2.80 m to 3.00 m before the first upright element of this two-stride double to help the horse take off at the correct place. If you reverse the grid, jumping the oxer first and then the upright, changing the rein, you should reduce the height of the jumps. This applies whenever you alter the order of the obstacles. A ground line placed in front of the last upright helps the horse to step under its centre of gravity on take-off.

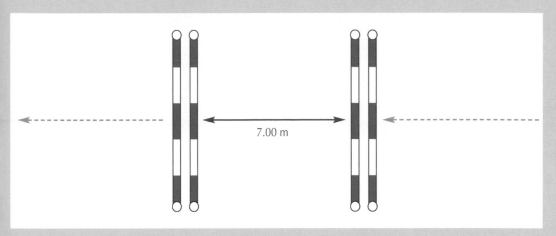

7.00 m

Example 9:
Generally, the distance here should be reduced. If you want to jump the oxers from both reins then they can be filled in on both sides with poles so they do not have to be completely rebuilt every time. The obstacles can then be jumped firstly on the left rein, then the right.
The horse should firstly be familiarised with changing the rein so that it remains relaxed.
The first small oxer increases the horse's bascule and encourages it to canter on fluently and with rhythm. This develops the required impulsion for the second larger oxer and encourages the horse to stretch and reach for the jump; a useful exercise for a horse that tightens its back.

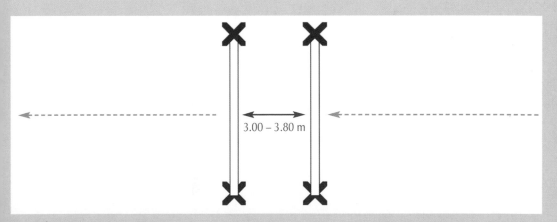

3.00 – 3.80 m

Example 10:
In-outs are useful for developing power, suppleness and rhythm. Also, most horses find them fun when they are suitable for their ability. A simple in-out can be raised to about 80 cm and can help young horses to become more proficient in their jumping ability. It can be built using cavaletti. The basic rule is: the smaller the jump, the smaller the distance.

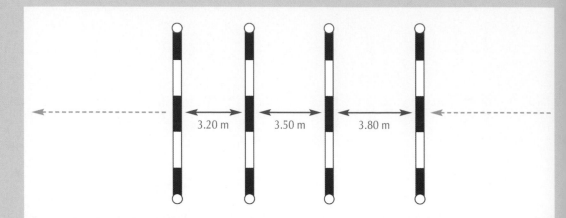

Example 11:
These three in-outs demand skill and power from the horse. Before building the grid like this make sure the horse can jump two in-outs without a problem. The distances decrease towards the last jump which should help to develop impulsion. If the horse has enough experience, the distances can all be the same. This is another exercises that can be jumped on each rein.

For the advanced handler

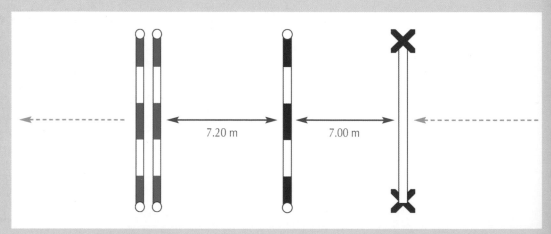

Example 12:
This is the classical jumping grid used for stallion testing in Germany for riding horses.
The upright after the cavaletto has a ground line and is only 60cm high. The last jump is built as an upright about 70cm high to start with, and is then built as a spread at a maximum height of 1.30m. This is to test the horse's ability, the power on take-off, the rhythm and balance of the canter, the bascule, and the leg technique.

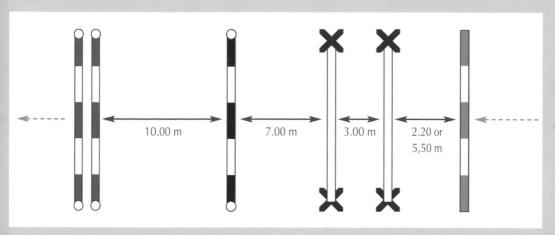

Example 13:
This grid, with an in-out at the beginning, is a good follow-on from example 3, page 58.
Power and concentration are improved even further. To improve attentiveness, a second pole
can be added 3.5 m after the second cavaletto.

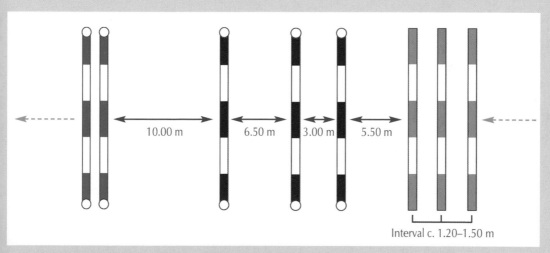

Example 14:
With this grid the smaller distances increase concentration. It is helpful if the horse is led in to the
trotting poles to ensure the horse trots over them. Starting with an in-out and the short distance to
the upright is an ideal way of calming down horses that tend to rush. Also this grid is useful gymnastic
work for the back and for developing rhythm. At a later stage the oxer can be raised and widened.

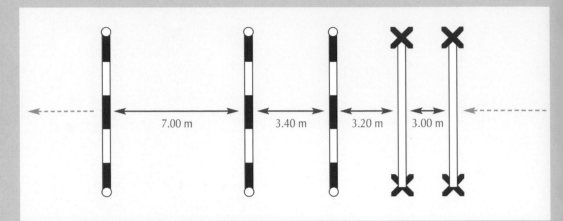

Example 15:
In-and-outs following each other are best made from cavaletti and small uprights, and are good for developing power and suppleness. When warming up only the first cavaletti are left as jumps, with the following jump poles laid on the ground.
It is important that the horse jumps energetically and does not have to stretch too much, so the distances should not be too wide. This grid is very good for developing rhythm.
Fore leg technique can also be improved with slightly narrower distances.

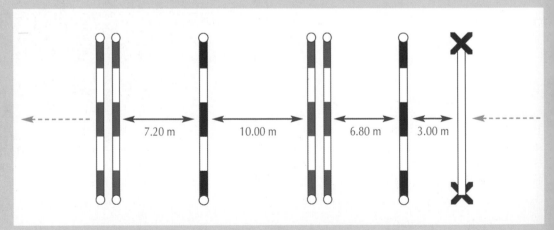

Example 16:
Here, the speed of reactions is improved. This grid is a difficult exercise because the horse must change between coming back on its hocks and stretching forwards.
As long as the grid is constructed to suit the horse the training improves the bascule and prepares the horse for a jumping course.

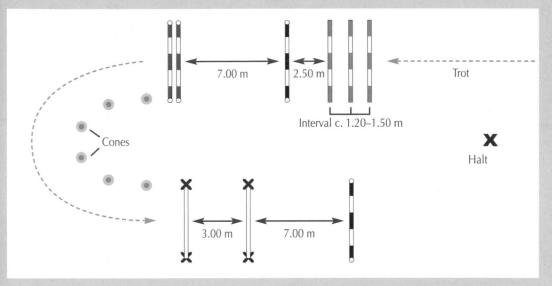

Example 17:

This is the first example of a round course to be jumped on the left hand. Before each attempt, the horse should be halted and then started again. The horse has to get used to the round course and it requires fitness and condition. Before you build large jumps on the second long side you should start with ground poles or cavaletti. The gymnastic effect is to distinguish between power and speed. Starting off quietly from trot over the in-out makes sure the horse has to change between acceleration and coming back on its hocks throughout the grid. The trotting poles on the round course give an opportunity to halt the horse and to start again from the trot.

Example 18:

The main purpose is for the horse to change between stretching and coming back on its hocks. This round course can be jumped on both reins and is good for stamina training and developing power. In an indoor school that is 25 metres wide and 60 metres long, this course can be built on the short side and will only take up 20 metres of the long side. This allows the rest of the school to be used for riding. Also, this free jumping exercise can be done alone. It should not be built too high. The oxer should be between 60–80 cm high, and up to 1 metre wide. A ground line set either side slightly away from the jump will make it more difficult. With the in-out cavaletti, start with two, then gradually increase the number.

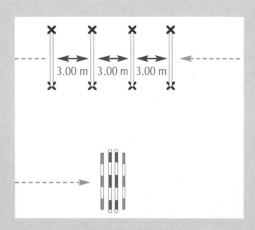

IMPROVING ATTITUDE, FAULT CORRECTIO

No-one is perfect, and this applies to horses as well as people. Mistakes can happen, even when free jumping is carefully and correctly carried out. The different temperaments of horses and variety of jump formation can affect day-to-day training, the effects of which are dealt with in this chapter. It is useful to know how to cope with different problems. It is not shameful to make mistakes, but it is important to learn from them. You can improve your horse's natural ability and attitude with correct, patient training. On the other hand, it is no surprise if the horse knocks a jump down at the first attempt. Even an experienced show jumper goes through phases in its training where it is not jumping at its best and requires some corrective work. With free jumping it is most important that mistakes and weaknesses are dealt with as and when they occur.

The 4-year-old part-bred Connemara mare, Annie, is over-eager, but not lacking in skill. She is not concentrating and jumps too fast and crookedly over the cavaletti with a plank on top. She concentrates better over a higher jump with two cavaletti, one on top of the other, with the plank as a ground line. (Note, it is not usual practice in the UK to stack cavaletti like this, in case they should fall. Plastic blocks or jump stands are a safer option.)

WHAT TO DO WHEN ...

... Your horse is careless and impetuous?
The next question you should ask yourself is:
- Is the horse unprepared either mentally
  or physically?
- Is it in pain?
- Is there another reason why this has happened?

Of course there are horses, many of which are show jumpers, that cannot wait to get over a grid. Others come in too fast due to inexperience or a lack of confidence. Observing the horse's eyes, its breathing, whether it is sweating, and its head carriage will give an indication as to why the horse is flying at the jumps. In this case, simplify the training. If this does not help and you are sure it is not a confidence issue, then try to improve the horse's concentration, for example by laying ground poles between the jumps or by using different fillers and jump materials.

It is important that the horse is given time to calm down and to jump properly, finding the correct take-off point.

....the horse does not want to jump?

Ask yourself the same questions as before when the horse comes in too fast. Many horses simply have no talent or do not enjoy jumping or free jumping, or have not been encouraged to do so in the past. Firstly do not ask too much of the horse. Work over ground poles or in-hand work can help the horse to get used to coloured poles. If the horse is afraid or cannot physically cope, give plenty of praise and encouragement. Staying calm is the best way to win the horse over. The horse must feel absolutely safe in order to jump or free-jump. It does not do the horse any harm to go back to basics. Fear and insecurity need to be vanquished and well-being needs to be increased.

....the horse takes off too early?

Is the distance right for this horse? Is the tempo correct? Horses that take off too early are often coming in too fast. This can be helped by placing a ground pole, or even better a small jump such as a cavaletti, before the obstacle one canter stride before the take-off point. Later you should let the horse find the take-off point for itself.

....the horse gets too close to the jump?

When the distance is correct, could the tempo be too slow for this horse? In this case encouragement should be given either with the voice or the whip. Firstly though, use a pole in front of the jump to give a clear ground line.

....the horse runs out?

It is quite normal for the horse to make a mistake at the first fence, and to run out at the next. If this is not due to inexperience, tiredness or pain, you should calmly try again. Remain calm, and make the exercise easier. Usually this happens if the jump is too high, so reduce the height. Eventually, change one obstacle at a time; make it higher, or make an upright fence into an oxer, or increase the distance slightly. Motivate the horse with kind words. Shouting, using the whip and charging around are definitely not the right way.

The 4-year-old Lusitano stallion Vao finds the jump difficult without a ground line. In canter he takes off far too early.

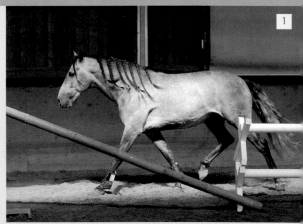

Once his eagerness has been curbed, and he comes into the jump from trot, he finds the correct take-off point at the first attempt.

The 8-year-old Irish pony, Juli, jumps in a good style, has the right attitude and is as supple as a cat. Coming in out of trot, she has lost some of her forwardness and takes off far too early several times, causing her to jump at full stretch, even over this small jump. She jumps much better from canter. (See photo page 7.)

… the horse stops dead?

The answer is clear: it could be too tired, not concentrating, have too little experience, ability or strength! When the horse cannot cope any more over a small obstacle it has no more strength, concentration or fitness for today. Try to finish on a good note before the horse reaches this state and make sure you are a better judge of your horse's fitness next time. If the horse is healthy, then find a way of improving its attitude. Try to find the solution, such as a tight back, and work on improving this.

… the horse has a poor foreleg technique?

If the horse lets its legs hang from the knees it needs to work with bigger distances between the obstacles. It must first learn to stretch and through that learn to lift the forelegs up more. Make sure you widen the distances gradually. Too much will have an adverse effect. If the horse hangs its cannon bones, this can be caused by poor back technique or lack of concentration. Here it can be helpful to place poles between the jumps or an in-out cavaletti after the jump, in the same way as an 'Aha' cross-country jump, to encourage a more positive muscular action.

For this gelding it is easier to flatten his back and rush than to remain in control. In this photo the three cavaletti are set close together. In the photo on page 71 although the jump is not in exactly the same phase, you can see how much more power from behind it takes to jump cavaletti placed close together than if they were set further apart, where he can, and should, stretch more.

… the horse jumps with a flat back?

In this situation it can help to shorten the distances in a combination, but keep them relative to the type of jump (oxer or upright). By shortening the distance to a parallel oxer you can encourage the horse to tuck its haunches under more, which will help the back to round. With inexperienced horses, it is better to start with an in-out to improve strength and suppleness.

… the horse does not jump boldly?

If the horse is not keen to jump or is tense, or jumps with a flat back it can help to use spreads and combinations. It is important that the horse finds the correct take-off point and that the distances are absolutely right for the horse and there are not too many jumps in the grid.

… the horse jumps too big?

For a young or inexperienced horse it is normal to jump too big at first as it has not yet learnt to gauge the height of the jumps. There are horses that are so keen and brave that they always over-jump. Some are so keen to jump big that they cannot be bothered with small jumps. By always jumping too exuberantly, they never learn to jump in good style.

With 5-year-old Faro you can see the benefits of free jumping very clearly. In the beginning he has little co-ordination.
In the first photo he jumps with difficulty on his forehand with his hind legs out behind and leaves his fore legs hanging.
A few attempts later however, he is making a much better effort.

A similar thing happens with his hindquarters. In the photo sequence in chapter 'Developing an eye for correct training' pages 46-47. you can see that he left his hind legs hanging initially. Here, in the first picture his hind quarters appear very cramped. In the last photo he does not tighten up through his withers on landing and his hind leg action is much better.

It can be helpful to find the horse's weak point and to work on that. It can be difficult for this type of horse to learn self-control, so it may be helpful to concentrate on improving suppleness.

... the horse is not interested and loses concentration?

Is it inexperienced or unprepared? It is acting out of character? Has it just eaten? It could be a result of a handling or a health problem. If it none of these, it may just be having an off-day. Motivation with the voice and a lot of praise may help to make the session more enjoyable. Sometimes nothing will help, and it is better to start afresh another day.

... the horse jumps crookedly?

Slight crookedness is not unusual. Jumping continually to the left can be caused by not building the grid properly. The distance may not suit the horse, or the last jump may be too near the corner, causing the horse to veer to the left because it is worried about approaching the corner.

If the horse jumps crookedly due to coming too fast over the last jump towards the corner, placing

The 13-year-old Levin loves free jumping so much that he jumps big and round even when he does not need to.

In the first photo the oxer is quite small.
He rounds his back very well but gives the jump a lot of room.

In the middle picture the oxer is higher and wider.
The first jump over it shows super front leg technique, but is slightly crooked.

In the third picture this is corrected by adding a cone on the left hand side of the ground line. The gelding then jumps straight, but still jumps big, though this is normal for him.

cones or wings after the last jump can help it to remain straight. Hosepipes, cones or cavaletti can be placed on the left side to help the horse jump straight on take-off. A ground rule is 'less is more'. A slight difference may be all that is needed – you will most likely find the solution by trial and error.

… the horse sweats excessively and breathes heavily?

Review your training programme. Have you done too much too soon? Is the horse ill perhaps? Take more breaks! It is best to halt the horse after each attempt for a reward and a short rest. Then lead it with a rope back to the beginning of the grid, where it can trot into the grid. In these short pauses the horse learns to relax both physically and mentally.

… the horse repeatedly lands in counter-canter?

If the horse repeatedly lands in counter-canter when free jumping on the left rein, make sure it is not in pain or injured. If not, you may have one of the few 'left-handed' horses. Only for these horses should you change the rein and jump on the right rein.

APPENDIX

ACKNOWLEDGEMENTS

Firstly I would like to thank Hakan Alp for his great support and carrying out the photo production. Hakan, who is a top classical trainer, also carries out free jumping at home. Without his help this manuscript would not have been so problem-free and quick to produce. Tremendous thanks go to the two proficient helpers, Maria Faltermeier and Janina Witowski. Special thanks go to Petra Gschwindt, for her support and hospitality at the Auenhof in Hebrontshausen near Munich, and also Claudia Geringer and Brigitte Schoob who lent us their horses Nellaun and Tessina. Many thanks to Leonie Schweiger and Karin Engelsberger.

Thank you also to Maxamilan Schreiner for his superb photographic work, it was a pleasure to work with him. Also I would like to thank my lecturer Anneke Bosse for supporting and encouraging my idea. Many thanks to Hilke Marx-Holena, without whom this book would not have come to fruition.

A hearty 'hello' to the two Haflingers, Tweety and Melodie, whose terrific synchronised jump over eight car tyres piled on top of each other made me think what a good idea this book would be.

Last but not least, I would like to thank all the horses shown in this book for their enthusiasm, concentration and their acceptance of our ideas and for increasing our knowledge a bit further.

FURTHER READING

Birgit van Damsen:
Improving Performance
Cadmos, 2008

Anne-Katrin Hagen:
From Flatwork to Jumping
Cadmos, 2004

Clarissa Busch:
Show Jumping Made Easy
Cadmos, 2003

Linda Weritz:
Horse Sense and Horsemanship
Cadmos, 2008

GLOSSARY

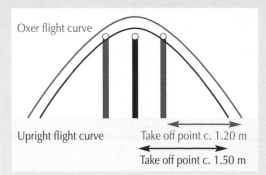

This is how the shape over the jump should look over an oxer and an upright about one metre high.

Ability:
The natural gift of the horse to judge the height of obstacles. This is closely linked to jumping style.

Bascule:
This refers to the curve of the horse's back over an obstacle. The vertebrae spread away from each other and the back muscles are stretched. Jumping with bascule is the healthiest way for the horse to jump. The amount of bascule is influenced somewhat by training, but it also depends on the horse's conformation and aptitude.

Big (also too big):
The horse jumps before reaching the ideal take-off point. It must then stretch more and make no mistakes. The shape over the jump is flatter.

Cavaletto:
A pole raised off the ground with a small cross attached at each end, or by laying it on plastic blocks. Cavaletti can be used in many ways – at the lowest height they can be used as ground poles with the advantage that they do not roll away. They can be turned to half-height (about 10 cm) or full – height (about 40 cm).

Clearing the jump:
You want the hindquarters to 'make it' over the jump, and they have to lift in order to do this. The ability to snap up the hindquarters is a sign of suppleness and helps to avoid jumping faults in a competition round.

Cross-pole:
Two poles are laid as a cross supported between two jump stands. Cross-poles are great to start with for both horse and rider as they are not too high and easy to jump. When free jumping, a cross-pole can help to bring a horse into the centre of the jump. Trot poles can be used on the approach to a cross-pole. They are less useful with horses that jump big, or those that tend to knock jumps down. If they are unfamiliar with cross-poles, some may find it difficult to judge the height and others may tend to jump too near the wall and go over the highest part.

Getting too close:
The horse jumps after the ideal take-off point. It gets far too close to the jump and the shape over the jump is steep and lacking in harmony.

Ground line:
A pole on the ground can be used to define a ground line. This is easier for the horse. High uprights can be made easier by using a ground line. A ground pole about 80 cm before the jump gives the horse the ideal take-off point.

Hanging, or not lifting, the front legs:
Ideally the horse should bend the knees and fetlocks sharply, and if possible, fold the front legs up underneath the belly. Many horses either leave one or both legs hanging from one or both joints, or bring them up late. This not only can cause jumping faults, but can be dangerous for both horse and rider. This could cause a fall or injury if this happens over an oxer or a solid fence.

In-out:
As it sounds – jumping in, then out straight away!
This is all in-out means. There is no canter stride
between the obstacles. The horse jumps in – often
from trot – jumps over the first obstacle, lands, and
directly takes off again.

Jumping style:
This describes the way in which the horse naturally
jumps, and how it behaves before and after the obstacle. Style affects how easy or difficult jumping
is for the horse.

Over-jumping (jumping big):
The horse gives the jump too much room. It jumps
higher than it needs. This is usually as a result of
either over-exuberance or inexperience.

Oxer:
A spread built with four jump stands. Normally, only
one pole is placed on the back two stands, while
an upright fence is built with the front pair of stands,
which should have fillers or be filled in with poles.
The back pole is always higher than the front one.
If both poles are the same height, then the fence is
described as a parallel. This can be jumped from
both sides.

Point of take-off:
The point before an obstacle that gives the opti-
mum bascule. With an upright of one metre high,
the ideal take-off point is about one and a half metres before the obstacle. With an oxer one metre
high and one metre wide, the ideal take-off point
is a good metre before the jump.

The higher the jump is the less room there is for
error when finding the ideal take-off point for op-
timum bascule and to clear the jump without making a mistake.

Spreads:
The horse must take into account the width as well
as the height of the jump. Examples are an oxer
and a triple bar.

Take-off:
The moment when the horse pushes off from the
ground. The more the horse flexes its haunches and
bends its hocks the better power it takes off with.
The flexibility and muscle tone of the haunches
have an influence over the horse's ability to push
off the ground.

The goal (successful jumping):
To jump successfully a horse should jump confidently on its own in a fluent and regular tempo,
clear the fence in style and with ease. Whether the
horse is free or ridden you should get the feeling
that the horse is flying effortlessly through the air.

The shape over a jump:
The shape, or arc, over an upright a good metre
high ideally needs a take-off point about two and
a half metres away. With an oxer the same height
and a metre wide the arc over the jump is over
three metres long and at its highest point, between
the two top poles, should be 10 cm higher than the
highest point of the oxer.

Triple-bar:
A minimum of three pairs of stands, or special
wings, that allow three poles to be set one behind
the other with the front one the lowest, and the
back one the highest.

Upright:
One or more poles are placed between two uprights. An upright without fillers is harder than one
that is filled in.

INDEX

OTHER CADMOS BOOKS

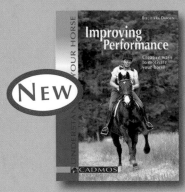

Birgit van Damsen
Improving Performance
This book discusses the possible causes of a lack of motivation – from physical problems, incorrect feeding, to permanent under- or over-demand of the horse, and it outlines solutions that can recover a seemingly hopeless situation.

Paperback, 80pp, fully illustrated
978-3-86127-956-3

Linda Weritz
Horse Sense and Horsemanship

Objective, sound and superbly elucidated, this book shows how mutual trust and respect are the key to a fulfilling partnership between man and horse. Every horse looks for and needs a trustworthy leader. Should a human in the eyes of the horse fail t inspire confidence, the horse is forced to assume responsibility for himself.

Paperback, 128pp, fully illustrated
978-3-86127-928-0

Hans-Peter Scheunemann
Starting out in Eventing

This book, by an experienced trainer, judge and course designer, describes all the the important requirements for safely improving your horse's ability in the cross-country phase. Training programms and instructions for coping with specific cross-country obstacles are included.

Paperback, 144pp, fully illustrated
978-3-86127-957-0

For further information:
Cadmos Books c/o Vicky Tischer
13 The Archers Way · BA6 9JB Glastonbury
Phone 01458 834 229 ·E-Mail info@cadmos.co.uk